Be a
DINOSAUR
DETECTIVE

Written by
DOUGAL DIXON

Illustrated by
STEVE LINGS

Lerner Publications Company   Minneapolis

This edition first published 1988 by Lerner Publications Company

Original edition copyright © 1987 by Templar Publishing Ltd.
First published in England by Purnells, a member of the BPCC Group.

This edition of this book is available in two bindings:
Library binding by Lerner Publications Company
Soft cover by First Avenue Editions
241 First Avenue North
Minneapolis, Minnesota 55401

Library of Congress Cataloging-in-Publication Data

Dixon, Dougal.
  Be a dinosaur detective.

  Includes index.
  Summary: Explores what dinosaurs were like and how they
lived based on evidence and clues found in fossils. In-
cludes related questions, instructions for making dinosaur
models, and other activities.
  1. Dinosaurs—Juvenile literature. [1. Dinosaurs]
I. Lings, Steve, ill. II. Title.
QE862.D5D53 1988   567.9'1   87-22740
ISBN 0-8225-0894-X (lib. bdg.)
ISBN 0-8225-9538-9 (pbk.)

Manufactured in the United States of America

5   6   7   8   9   10   –   P/JR   –   01   00   99   98   97   96   95   94

CONTENTS

Fossil follies

Pretend you lived over 200 years ago. You would never have heard of fossils, as no one knew what they were. Imagine you were walking along a beach, where the cliffs were being worn away by the sea – or scrambling in a mountain gully where a waterfall tumbled down a hillside – and you found one of these strange things.

This is a fossil, today called an ammonite. What would you think it was just by looking at it?

The best guess that people 200 years ago could come up with was that these were the remains of long-dead snakes.

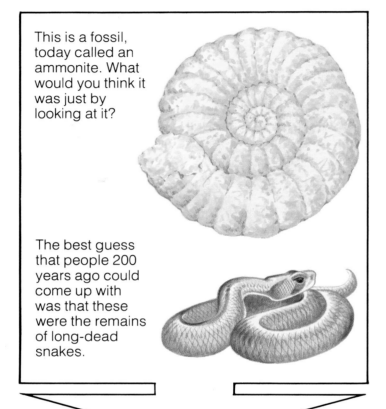

This peculiar looking thing is a skull. No one was in any doubt about that.

But the "experts" from 200 years ago guessed wrongly about the skull's owner. They thought it belonged to a giant Cyclops (a one-eyed man in ancient stories).

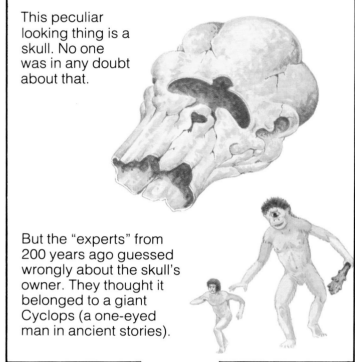

In fact

Today we know that ammonites are the coiled shells of octopus-like animals.

In fact

Nowadays it is taken for granted that the skull belonged to a type of elephant called a mammoth. The big hole in the middle of the "forehead" is not an eye hole, but the nostril where the trunk was attached.

These bullet-like objects are made of rock. Could you work out what they used to be?

One common idea 200 years ago was that these mysterious things were in fact thunderbolts.

This rock covered in fossil sea shells was found by a waterfall high on a mountain. It was nowhere near the sea.

As they were found so far away from the sea, people thought that the shells were left on the mountain by the great Flood mentioned in the Bible.

In fact

The "thunderbolts" were actually the fossilized shells of squid-like animals. These fossils are called belemnites.

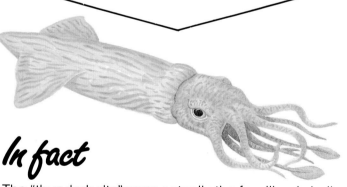

In fact

The shell-covered rock was found high above the sea because the mountains themselves were formed from rocks that once made up the sea bed. They have been forced into new forms by the natural actions of the Earth's crust.

False starts

200 years ago people didn't know much about the world around them. Nowadays there is a solid background of science which we use to help us come up with new theories. Most scientific ideas about prehistoric life come from fossils – like those shown on these two pages. Fossils are the remains of dead animals and plants preserved in rock for millions of years.

When people started to take fossils seriously, they encountered a few problems. In 1725 these fake fossils were made out of clay by some university professors and students who wanted to fool another professor. The poor man was confused for years!

This skeleton of a "sea-serpent" was put together by a hoaxer in 1846. He made it out of the fossil bones of some whales. Many great scientists were fooled by it.

The world of the past

How do we know what the world was like a very long time ago? Well, we can look at the rocks. There are three different types of rocks. One type is formed when hot molten lava from inside the Earth cools and becomes hard. Another forms when an already existing rock is squeezed or "cooked" inside the Earth and turns into something new. The third type forms from sand and mud which piles up on a sea bed or river bed. Let's look at this third type here. It is called "sedimentary rock."

Make some sedimentary rock

2. Now pour in a layer of mud mixed with plaster-of-Paris. Add a layer of gravel and another layer of sand. These layers should be mixed with dry plaster-of-Paris too.

1. Take a large plastic jar and pour a couple of inches of dry sand mixed with the same amount of plaster-of-Paris into it.

In the real world, the first layer of sand may have formed on a river bed.

Then the river may have been flooded by the sea. The mud layer would then have formed on top of the sand at the bottom of the sea.

Next, the sea may have dried up, and a pebble beach may have formed to make yet another new layer.

Rock formation
Here are some pictures of rocks that show how they were formed.

This rock formed from clay in a pond. The pond dried up and the clay cracked in the hot sun. You can now see the shapes of these cracks in the rock.

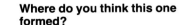

Where do you think this one formed?

These great curved beds are actually fossil sand dunes. This shows that the sandstone in this cliff was once a desert.

3.

Look at how the mass has formed different layers. While you are pouring these layers, drop in a few seashells as well. Then add water, until all the layers are saturated. Leave it to set for a couple of days.

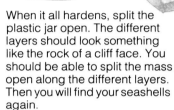

4.

When it all hardens, split the plastic jar open. The different layers should look something like the rock of a cliff face. You should be able to split the mass open along the different layers. Then you will find your seashells again.

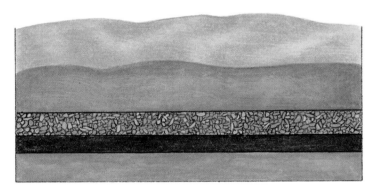

Finally, a desert may have spread gradually to cover the whole area. Millions of years later, water may have seeped through all these layers, and left minerals stuck between the grains – just like your plaster-of-Paris did. These minerals would have cemented the grains into rock.

Any animals that died in the river, the sea, the shore, or the desert would have left their bones and shells in this rock. Over millions of years these would have been turned into fossils.

CLIFF CLUES

Here is a cliff made from the rocks that were laid down by the real-life ancient river, sea, shore, and desert. We have left holes for the fossils. **Where do you think you would find the oldest rock? At the top or the bottom?**

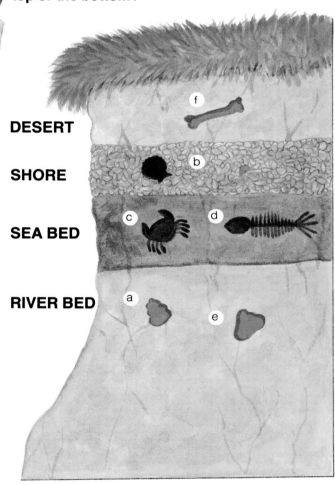

DESERT

SHORE

SEA BED

RIVER BED

Here are the kinds of fossils that we would expect to find in the different layers, or beds, of rocks. **See if you can match them to their rock types**.

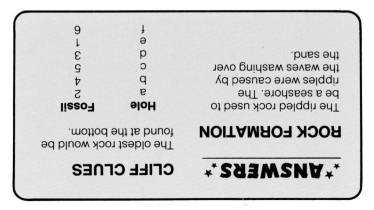

1. Skull of a frog.

2. Water snail.

3. Fish skeleton.

4. Cockle shell.

5. Crab shell.

6. Lizard bone.

Animals through the ages

The Earth is old, older than you can possibly imagine. In fact, it is about 4,500,000,000 (four billion, five hundred million) years old. Life probably started on the Earth about 3,500,000,000 (three billion, five hundred million) years ago. The first living things were only tiny soft blobs. It was not until about 570,000,000 (five hundred and seventy million) years ago that animals with hard shells and skeletons appeared. This is how old the

oldest identifiable fossils are.

All these figures are a bit much to take in. So geologists have split up the Earth's history into chunks called **eras** and **periods** and have given them different names – just as we split up a year into months with different names. The whole thing together is called the **geological column**. All the different changes that take place – like new plants and animals appearing – are together called **evolution**.

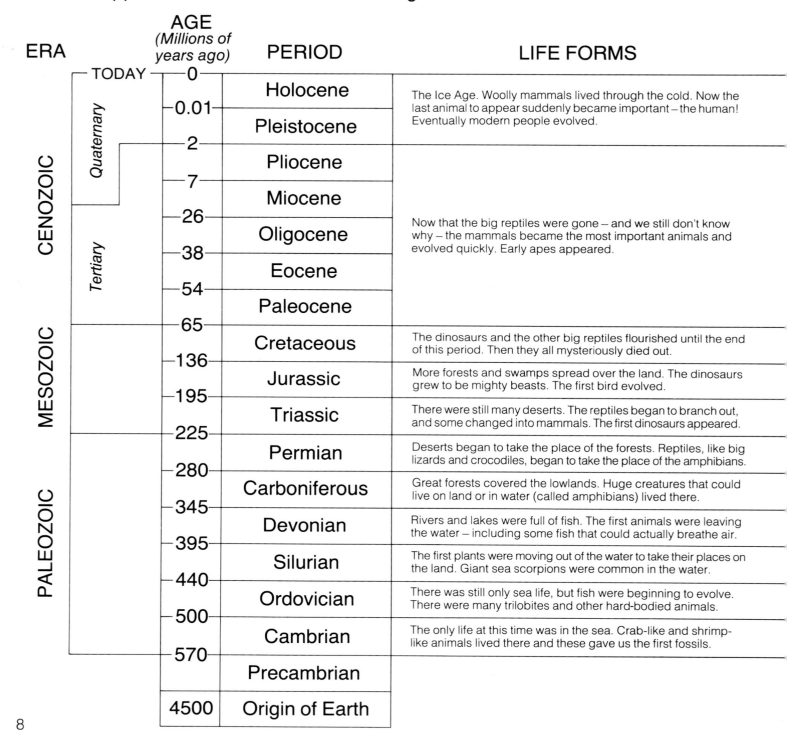

ERA		AGE (Millions of years ago)	PERIOD	LIFE FORMS
CENOZOIC	Quaternary	TODAY — 0	Holocene	The Ice Age. Woolly mammals lived through the cold. Now the last animal to appear suddenly became important – the human! Eventually modern people evolved.
		0.01	Pleistocene	
		2	Pliocene	Now that the big reptiles were gone – and we still don't know why – the mammals became the most important animals and evolved quickly. Early apes appeared.
	Tertiary	7	Miocene	
		26	Oligocene	
		38	Eocene	
		54	Paleocene	
		65		
MESOZOIC			Cretaceous	The dinosaurs and the other big reptiles flourished until the end of this period. Then they all mysteriously died out.
		136	Jurassic	More forests and swamps spread over the land. The dinosaurs grew to be mighty beasts. The first bird evolved.
		195	Triassic	There were still many deserts. The reptiles began to branch out, and some changed into mammals. The first dinosaurs appeared.
		225		
PALEOZOIC			Permian	Deserts began to take the place of the forests. Reptiles, like big lizards and crocodiles, began to take the place of the amphibians.
		280	Carboniferous	Great forests covered the lowlands. Huge creatures that could live on land or in water (called amphibians) lived there.
		345	Devonian	Rivers and lakes were full of fish. The first animals were leaving the water – including some fish that could actually breathe air.
		395	Silurian	The first plants were moving out of the water to take their places on the land. Giant sea scorpions were common in the water.
		440	Ordovician	There was still only sea life, but fish were beginning to evolve. There were many trilobites and other hard-bodied animals.
		500	Cambrian	The only life at this time was in the sea. Crab-like and shrimp-like animals lived there and these gave us the first fossils.
		570	Precambrian	
		4500	Origin of Earth	

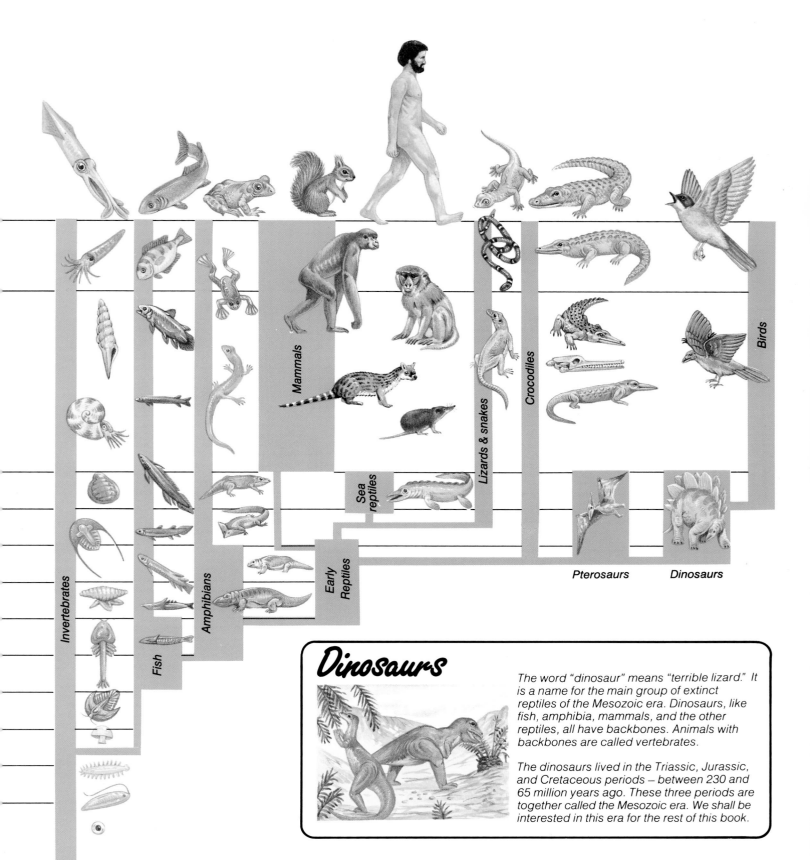

Invertebrates

Fish

Amphibians

Mammals

Early Reptiles

Sea reptiles

Lizards & snakes

Crocodiles

Pterosaurs

Dinosaurs

Birds

Dinosaurs

The word "dinosaur" means "terrible lizard." It is a name for the main group of extinct reptiles of the Mesozoic era. Dinosaurs, like fish, amphibia, mammals, and the other reptiles, all have backbones. Animals with backbones are called vertebrates.

The dinosaurs lived in the Triassic, Jurassic, and Cretaceous periods — between 230 and 65 million years ago. These three periods are together called the Mesozoic era. We shall be interested in this era for the rest of this book.

The big skeleton

A scientist interested in dinosaurs would be very lucky to find a complete dinosaur skeleton. Usually dinosaur remains are just made up of scattered bones. And even if the skeleton is complete, the bones will usually be all jumbled up. You can see the mixed-up remains of one complete dinosaur skeleton on this page. You will see that these remains also include the skull. The skull is usually missing from real skeletons. That is because dinosaurs'

skulls were so lightly built that they often broke before they could become fossils.

Trace over the shapes of the pieces. Then draw them on thick paper or thin cardboard and piece the bits together to make a whole dinosaur. Once you have assembled your skeleton, jumble it all up again. Then throw half the pieces away and try to build it again. This is more like the problem given to scientists by real skeletons that they dig out of the rocks.

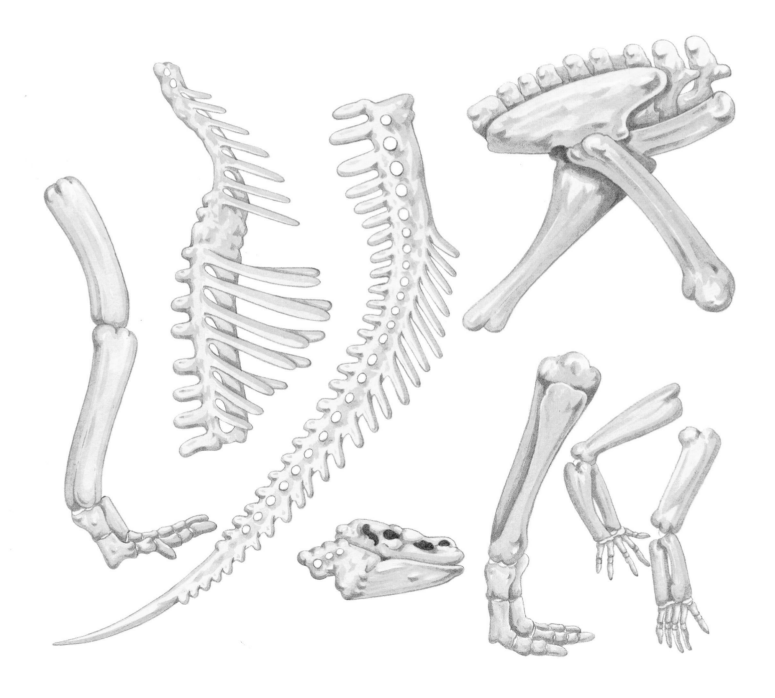

A fossil poser

Which of the dinosaurs shown here are most likely to become fossilized? **Can you guess why?**

Skeleton skills

Here are some jumbled-up dinosaur skeletons, just as they were found in the rocks. **See if you can identify them from the pictures in the rest of the book.**

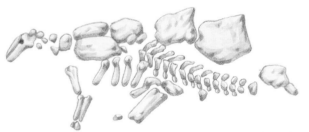

This one was found in the late Jurassic rocks in North America. Look at the broad plates lying near the backbone as a clue to its name.

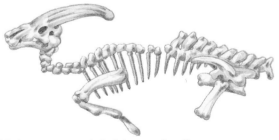

This is a very good skeleton, as fossil skeletons go, even though only half of it remains. It is from the late Cretaceous and was found in North America. Notice the great curving crest on the skull.

Dancing dinosaurs?

Sometimes dinosaur remains consist only of footprints. Here is a trail of fossil footprints belonging to two dinosaurs. **Can you tell what happened?**

★ ANSWERS ★

A FOSSIL POSER
The dinosaurs in or near the water would be the most likely to become fossils if they died. This is because their bodies would be covered in mud which would harden and, in time, preserve the bones as stone.

SKELETON SKILLS
The Jurassic skeleton belonged to a *Stegosaurus*. The late Cretaceous skeleton used to be a *Parasaurolophus*.

DANCING DINOSAURS?
One theory about these footprints says that the owner of the small feet was caught by the large-footed dinosaur and turned into a meal. Of course, you may have other ideas.

Meat-eating dinosaurs

Everything that we know about dinosaurs – and all other prehistoric animals – is deduced from the evidence and clues found in their fossils.

The different shapes of dinosaur bodies and the bones that they are made from tell us a lot about their way of life.

Here and on the following pages, you can find out all about what meat-eating dinosaurs were like and how they used to live.

TEETH

The teeth of a meat-eating dinosaur were sharp and often had edges like those on a saw, because they had to cut through meat. This is a tooth from the largest meat-eater – *Tyrannosaurus*.

SKULL

A dinosaur's skull was full of holes. This kept it light. A meat-eater's skull was made from many pieces, loosely held together. This meant that it could change shape slightly to let the animal swallow large chunks of meat. **Which of the dinosaurs shown on pages 14 and 15 owned this horned skull?**

ARMS

The arms, called forelimbs, were usually used to hold prey.

This tiny limb has only two fingers. It belonged to the biggest meat-eater of them all. Its arms could only have been used to push the dinosaur off the ground when it was getting to its feet. **Look at pages 14 and 15 to find out who the dinosaur was.**

This enormous arm is from a meat-eating dinosaur called *Deinocheirus*. It is 8.5 feet (2.6 meters) long. We don't know anything about the rest of its body.

Make a meat-eating dinosaur

Get some modeling clay about the size of a tennis ball, one long pencil and two short ones, a spring clothespin, and two used matchsticks.

1. Take a large lump of modeling clay and mold it into a ball. Now stick the two short pencils into it. These are the dinosaur's legs. Put a small clay "foot" on the end of each pencil.

3. Your dinosaur's jaws make it very heavy at the front. You'll probably find that it falls over. To make it balance, the meat-eater needs a tail at the back.

2. The teeth and jaws are very important. The dinosaur used these to kill its food. The clothespin makes the dinosaur's jaws.

4. Finally, use the matchsticks to make the dinosaur's forelimbs. Stick them into the front, near the head.

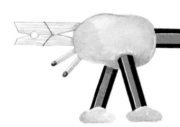

All the meat-eating dinosaurs were built to this design – but not out of modeling clay! All the different meat-eating dinosaurs shown on the following pages have this basic shape.

LEGS

The two hind legs of the meat-eating dinosaur carried all its weight.
See if you can match the two straight legs on the right with their owners, shown on pages 14 and 15.

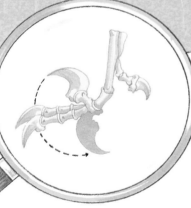

Here is a foot used for killing. That huge claw on the second toe must have been used to slash the dinosaur's victim to death. The other big toes were used for walking.

This leg is long and slim. We know it must have belonged to a swift-running animal, because it looks like the leg of an ostrich.

This leg is about 13 feet (4 m) long. Look how thick the bones are. It must have supported an enormous animal. It had three huge toes that touched the ground and one small one that did not.

★ ANSWERS ★

SKULL
Ceratosaurus owned the horned skull.

ARMS
The little arms belonged to *Tyrannosaurus*.

LEGS
Dromiceiomimus used to run with the slim leg, while *Tyrannosaurus* stood on the giant one.

13

Famous meat-eaters

This is how big you would be compared to these dinosaurs. Imagine what it would be like to have lived when they were around!

Tyrannosaurus (tyrant lizard). As far as we know, this was the biggest meat-eater of the lot. It was 40 feet (12 m) long and lived in North America and China in late Cretaceous times.

Food See if you can guess which of the meat-eating dinosaurs on these pages ate these different types of meat.

Dead animals Probably eaten by dinosaurs too large and slow to catch live food.

Large live animals Eaten by dinosaurs that had special big claws that could kill them.

Smaller live animals These would have been caught and eaten by the powerful hunters which were between 17 and 33 feet (5 and 10 m) long.

Lizards and insects These must have been eaten by the smallest meat-eaters.

Eggs Meat-eating dinosaurs with no teeth may have eaten other dinosaurs' eggs.

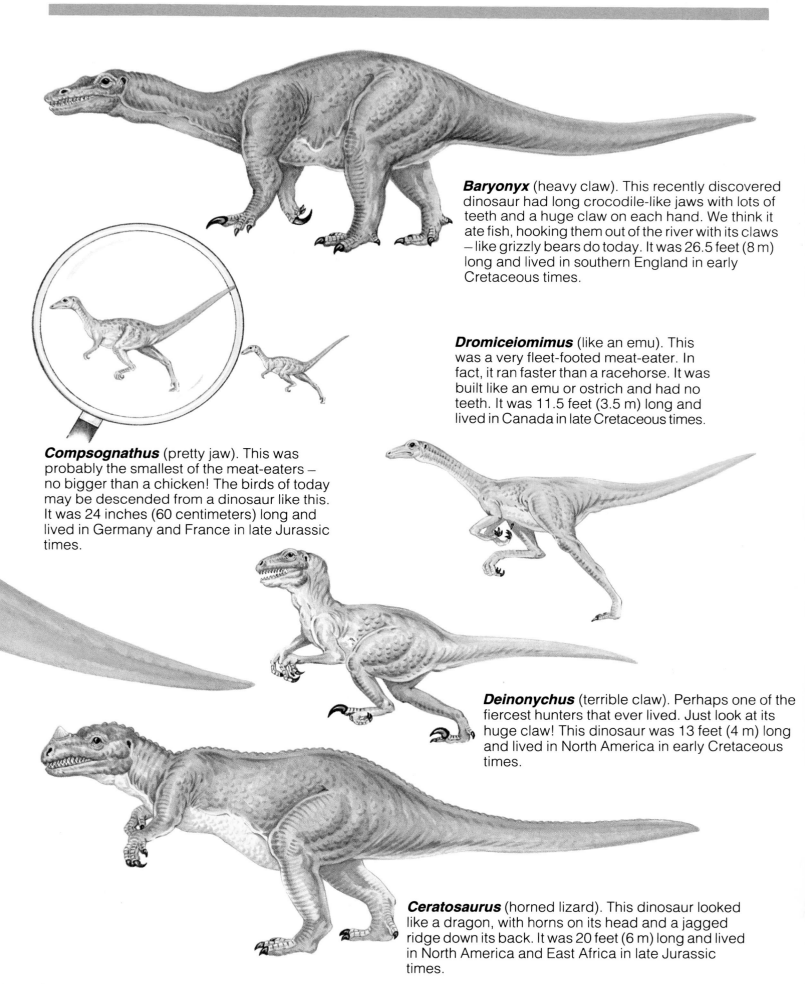

Baryonyx (heavy claw). This recently discovered dinosaur had long crocodile-like jaws with lots of teeth and a huge claw on each hand. We think it ate fish, hooking them out of the river with its claws — like grizzly bears do today. It was 26.5 feet (8 m) long and lived in southern England in early Cretaceous times.

Dromiceiomimus (like an emu). This was a very fleet-footed meat-eater. In fact, it ran faster than a racehorse. It was built like an emu or ostrich and had no teeth. It was 11.5 feet (3.5 m) long and lived in Canada in late Cretaceous times.

Compsognathus (pretty jaw). This was probably the smallest of the meat-eaters — no bigger than a chicken! The birds of today may be descended from a dinosaur like this. It was 24 inches (60 centimeters) long and lived in Germany and France in late Jurassic times.

Deinonychus (terrible claw). Perhaps one of the fiercest hunters that ever lived. Just look at its huge claw! This dinosaur was 13 feet (4 m) long and lived in North America in early Cretaceous times.

Ceratosaurus (horned lizard). This dinosaur looked like a dragon, with horns on its head and a jagged ridge down its back. It was 20 feet (6 m) long and lived in North America and East Africa in late Jurassic times.

Long-necked plant-eaters

The dinosaurs were some of the largest animals that ever lived. The largest dinosaurs were all plant-eaters. They had enormously heavy bodies, which were supported on massive legs like tree trunks, and they all had long necks and tails.

SKULLS

Plant-eating dinosaurs had two main types of skull. The first was long and thin with teeth like a comb. The second was box-like and had teeth like chisels. **Can you match up the shapes of these skulls with the dinosaurs shown on the following pages?**

(a)

(b)

NECK VERTEBRAE

The bones in the neck – called vertebrae – were very large. They had to be to hold all the muscles that supported the neck. This bone is longer than an arm. It belonged to a very tall dinosaur. **Which one do you think it belonged to?**

A HALF-WAY STAGE?

This skeleton belongs to a dinosaur called *Anchisaurus*. It lived in North America in the Triassic period – before the long-necked plant-eaters evolved. Scientists think that it sometimes walked on its hind legs and sometimes on all fours, and many believe that it ate both meat and plants. Animals like this may have been the ancestors of the big plant-eaters.

THE FEET

The feet of a long-necked plant-eater were as big as serving trays. They had to support an animal weighing as much as a railway engine. They were probably built like elephants' feet, with a thick fibrous cushion beneath the toes to take the weight. There were five toes on each foot. The front foot usually had a big claw, and the back foot had either two or three big claws.

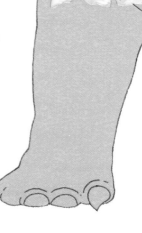

★ **ANSWERS** *★*

NECK VERTEBRAE
It belonged to *Brachiosaurus*.

TAIL VERTEBRAE
It belonged to *Diplodocus*.

SKULLS
Skull (a) came from a *Diplodocus*, while skull (b) belonged to a *Camarasaurus*.

EGGS
Eggs would have been laid by plant-eating dinosaurs when moving, to stop them piling up and crushing the ones on the bottom.

Make a big plant-eating dinosaur

1. Start with your model meat-eating dinosaur that you made on page 13. The plant-eating dinosaurs were evolved from small meat-eating dinosaurs.

2. Plant-eating animals need much more gut than meat-eating ones. This is because plants need more digestion than meat. Plant-eating dinosaurs therefore need bigger bodies. Make the body of your model longer, by adding more clay.

3. Your dinosaur will fall over because its tail will not be able to balance it any more. Make the front legs much bigger (using two more half pencils) so that your dinosaur can stand on four feet.

4. A plant-eating dinosaur will not need great big jaws and huge teeth to kill with. Take the "jaws" away and make a small head from clay. If you stick this straight onto the body the animal will not be able to reach its food. So use some more modeling clay to give it a long-reaching neck.

The big plant-eating dinosaurs were built to this design. All the plant-eating dinosaurs shown on pages 18 and 19 have this basic shape.

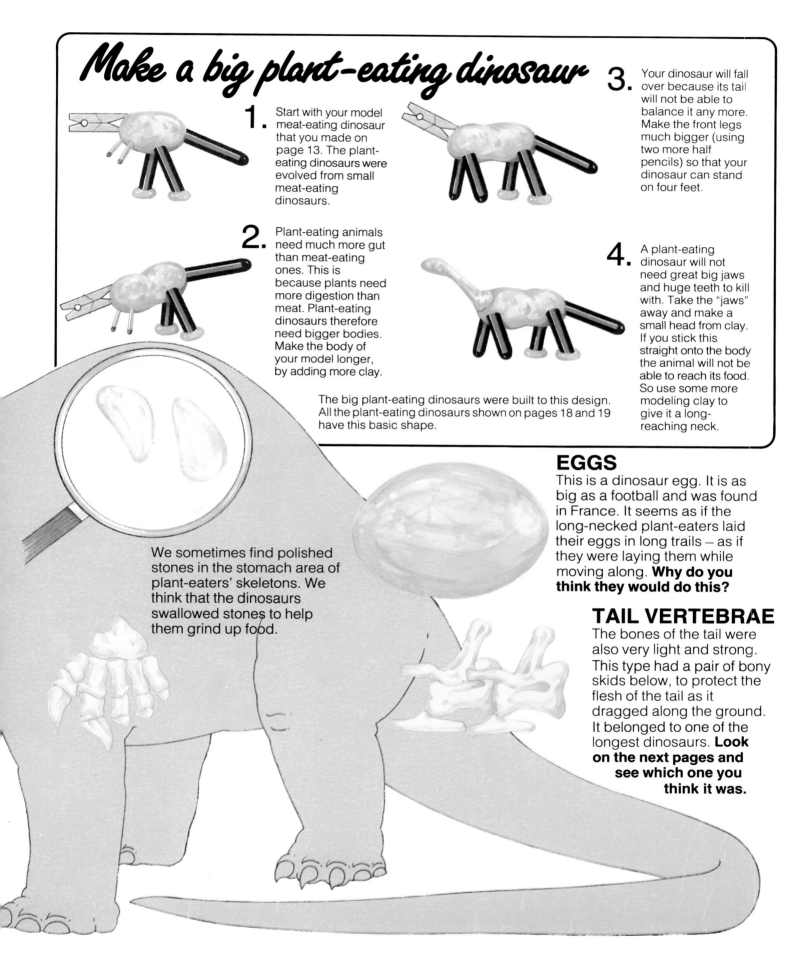

We sometimes find polished stones in the stomach area of plant-eaters' skeletons. We think that the dinosaurs swallowed stones to help them grind up food.

EGGS

This is a dinosaur egg. It is as big as a football and was found in France. It seems as if the long-necked plant-eaters laid their eggs in long trails – as if they were laying them while moving along. **Why do you think they would do this?**

TAIL VERTEBRAE

The bones of the tail were also very light and strong. This type had a pair of bony skids below, to protect the flesh of the tail as it dragged along the ground. It belonged to one of the longest dinosaurs. **Look on the next pages and see which one you think it was.**

17

Famous long-necked plant-eaters

Most of these animals were absolutely enormous. These tiny figures show the size that you would have been beside them.

Diplodocus (with two beams). Its name comes from the two bony skids that protected the tail as it dragged along the ground. At 89 feet (27 m), it was one of the longest of the dinosaurs, although quite lightly built. It lived at the same time and in the same place as *Apatosaurus*.

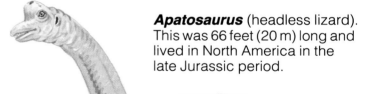

Mamenchisaurus (lizard from Mamenchi). This was like *Diplodocus*, but it had an extremely long neck — about half the length of the animal. It was about the same length as *Diplodocus* and lived in China in the late Jurassic.

Bone puzzles

(a)

We don't usually find complete dinosaur skeletons — usually just scattered bones. Here are some incomplete skeletons as they were found. See if you can match them up to the animals on this page.

(b)

Apatosaurus (headless lizard). This was 66 feet (20 m) long and lived in North America in the late Jurassic period.

Brachiosaurus (arm lizard). This was one of the tallest of the dinosaurs, reaching up to the height of the top windows of a three-storey house. Its forelimbs were longer than its hind limbs, which is unusual for these dinosaurs. It lived in North America and East Africa in the late Jurassic period.

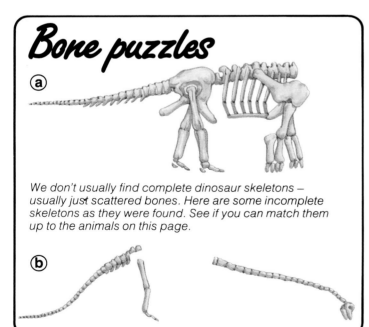

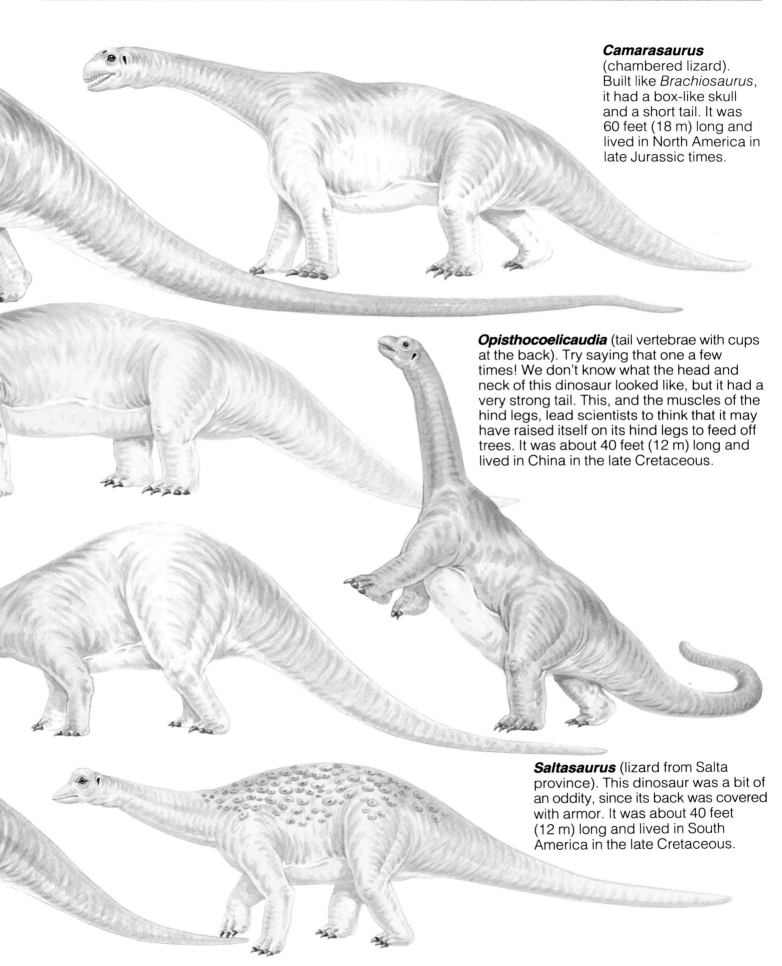

Camarasaurus (chambered lizard). Built like *Brachiosaurus*, it had a box-like skull and a short tail. It was 60 feet (18 m) long and lived in North America in late Jurassic times.

Opisthocoelicaudia (tail vertebrae with cups at the back). Try saying that one a few times! We don't know what the head and neck of this dinosaur looked like, but it had a very strong tail. This, and the muscles of the hind legs, lead scientists to think that it may have raised itself on its hind legs to feed off trees. It was about 40 feet (12 m) long and lived in China in the late Cretaceous.

Saltasaurus (lizard from Salta province). This dinosaur was a bit of an oddity, since its back was covered with armor. It was about 40 feet (12 m) long and lived in South America in the late Cretaceous.

Two-footed plant-eaters

SKULL SKILLS

Sometimes the dinosaur's "beak" was quite broad, like a duck bill, and was backed up by huge batteries of grinding teeth. Some dinosaurs evolved these duck bills to help them gather up and eat big mouthfuls of plants. Some of the duck-billed dinosaurs had strange crests on their heads. Here are two duck-billed dinosaur's skulls. **Can you match them up with the animals shown on the following pages?**

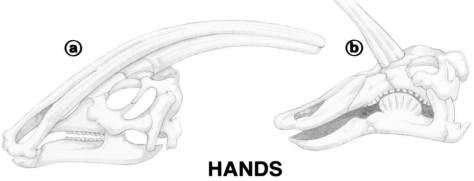

HANDS

Some of the plant-eating dinosaurs had five fingers on each hand, but those known as the duck-bills had only four. *Iguanodon* had five fingers. Its first, the thumb, was a huge spike. **What do you think it was used for?**

The duck-bill's hands may have been paddle-like, with webs of skin between the fingers. **What could this have been used for?**

LIFESTYLES

Hypsilophodon was a small two-footed plant-eater. It was about the size of a tree kangaroo. This led some paleontologists (fossil experts) to think that it must have climbed trees. We now know that it could not, as its feet were the wrong shape.

The duck-bills had a family life. We know this because we have found nests, still containing fossil babies. The nests were muddy heaps, like those of flamingos. These dinosaurs may have lived in flocks, too, just like flamingos do today.

TEETH

The two-legged plant-eaters had teeth that chopped and ground up their plant food. They also had cheek pouches to hold the food while they were chewing it. The hollows in the side of some skulls show where the cheek pouches were. They also had a beak at the front of their mouth. Sometimes the skull was narrow and the beak was quite pointed, like *Iguanodon's*, shown here.

HIPS

This is a hip bone from a two-legged plant-eater. There would have been a space beneath to hold the big gut needed to digest plant food.

Make a *two-footed plant-eater*

Remember the long-necked plant-eaters? We found out from looking at them that a plant-eating animal needs a big gut. The two-legged plant-eaters, however, were designed quite differently. You can see how by making another model. Get a big lump of modeling clay to use as the body, some pencils for the legs and tail, and two used matches.

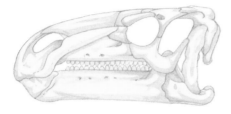

1. Stick two pencils into the sides of the modeling clay to make the hind legs. The heavy body should hang between the legs, not in front of them. The two-legged plant-eaters had special hip bones to let their bodies work in this way.

2. Now you can add the matches to make the short forearms and a small lump of modeling clay for the small head. Finish off the dinosaur with a pencil to make the stiff tail which balanced it all.

FEET

The two-footed plant-eaters' feet were usually three toed. They looked like birds' feet. They also looked a bit like the feet of the meat-eaters, so the footprints of the two types of dinosaur are often confused. However, one type all had blunt hooves on the toes, while the other had sharp claws. **Which dinosaurs do you think had which feet?**

TAIL BONES

The vertebrae of these dinosaurs' tails were firmly lashed together by bony tendons (above). This shows that the tails were held stiff and straight.

Famous two-footed plant-eaters

Many of the two-footed plant-eaters were quite small, but some were very big. They are shown to the same scale on this page. Here you are again, compared with them.

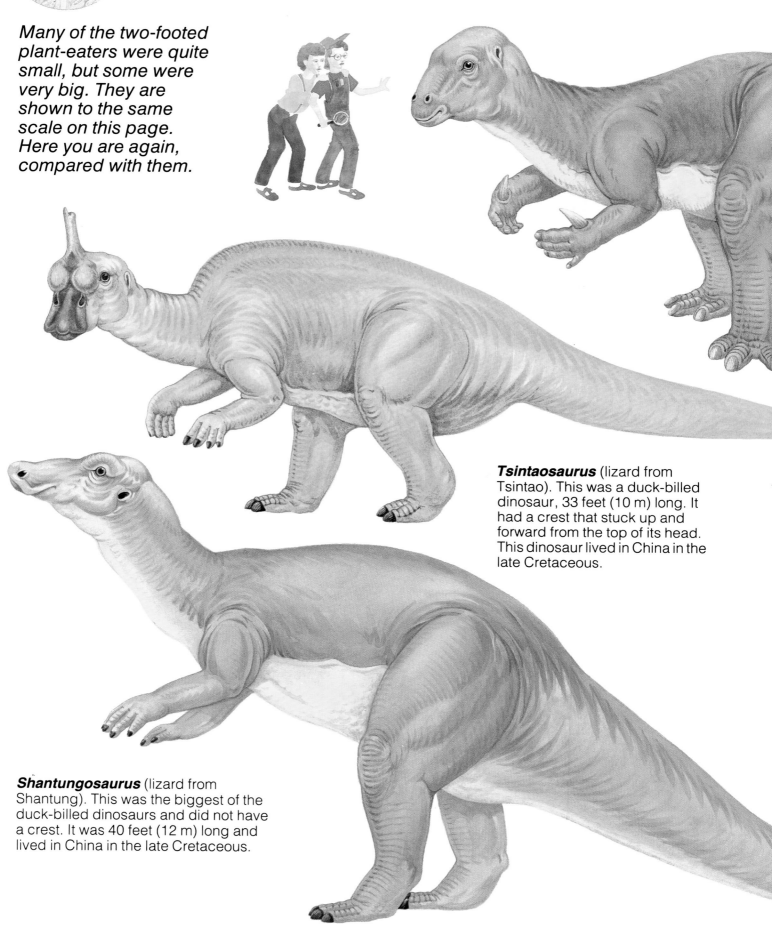

Tsintaosaurus (lizard from Tsintao). This was a duck-billed dinosaur, 33 feet (10 m) long. It had a crest that stuck up and forward from the top of its head. This dinosaur lived in China in the late Cretaceous.

Shantungosaurus (lizard from Shantung). This was the biggest of the duck-billed dinosaurs and did not have a crest. It was 40 feet (12 m) long and lived in China in the late Cretaceous.

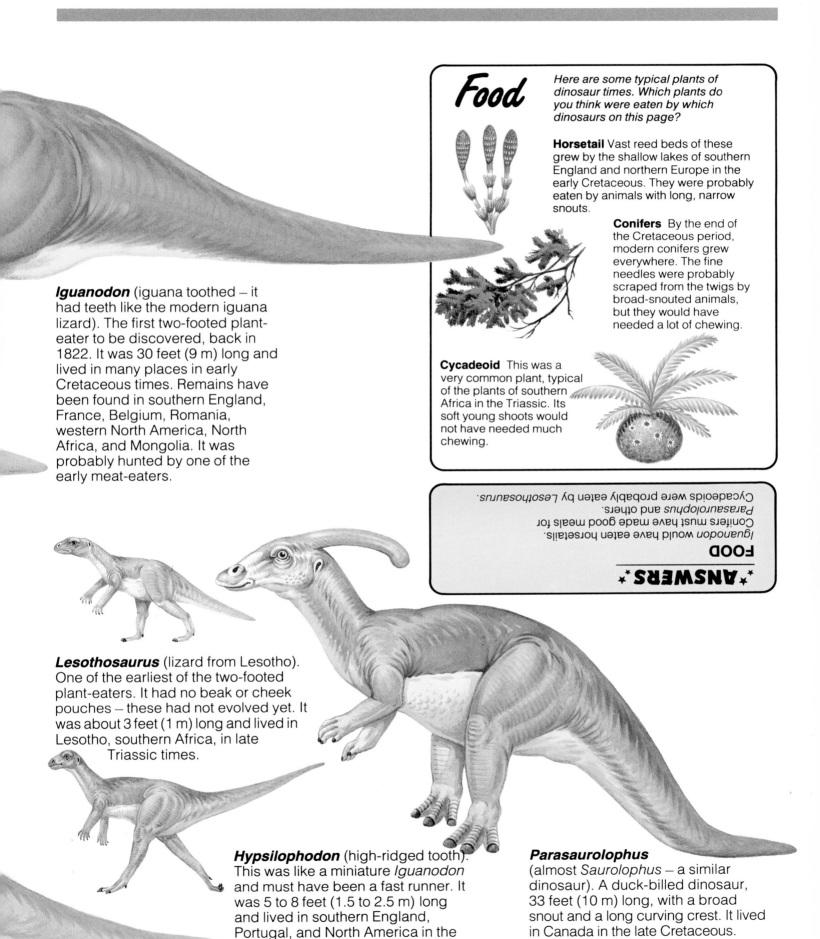

Iguanodon (iguana toothed – it had teeth like the modern iguana lizard). The first two-footed plant-eater to be discovered, back in 1822. It was 30 feet (9 m) long and lived in many places in early Cretaceous times. Remains have been found in southern England, France, Belgium, Romania, western North America, North Africa, and Mongolia. It was probably hunted by one of the early meat-eaters.

Food

Here are some typical plants of dinosaur times. Which plants do you think were eaten by which dinosaurs on this page?

Horsetail Vast reed beds of these grew by the shallow lakes of southern England and northern Europe in the early Cretaceous. They were probably eaten by animals with long, narrow snouts.

Conifers By the end of the Cretaceous period, modern conifers grew everywhere. The fine needles were probably scraped from the twigs by broad-snouted animals, but they would have needed a lot of chewing.

Cycadeoid This was a very common plant, typical of the plants of southern Africa in the Triassic. Its soft young shoots would not have needed much chewing.

★ ANSWERS ★

FOOD

Iguanodon would have eaten horsetails.

Conifers must have made good meals for *Parasaurolophus* and others.

Cycadeoids were probably eaten by *Lesothosaurus*.

Lesothosaurus (lizard from Lesotho). One of the earliest of the two-footed plant-eaters. It had no beak or cheek pouches – these had not evolved yet. It was about 3 feet (1 m) long and lived in Lesotho, southern Africa, in late Triassic times.

Hypsilophodon (high-ridged tooth). This was like a miniature *Iguanodon* and must have been a fast runner. It was 5 to 8 feet (1.5 to 2.5 m) long and lived in southern England, Portugal, and North America in the early Cretaceous.

Parasaurolophus (almost *Saurolophus* – a similar dinosaur). A duck-billed dinosaur, 33 feet (10 m) long, with a broad snout and a long curving crest. It lived in Canada in the late Cretaceous.

Armored plant-eaters

The armored plant-eaters had the same sort of hips as the two-footed plant-eaters, but they walked on all fours since they didn't need to run away from their enemies. They could protect themselves in other ways, as you can see here. Look on the following pages to find the answers to the questions.

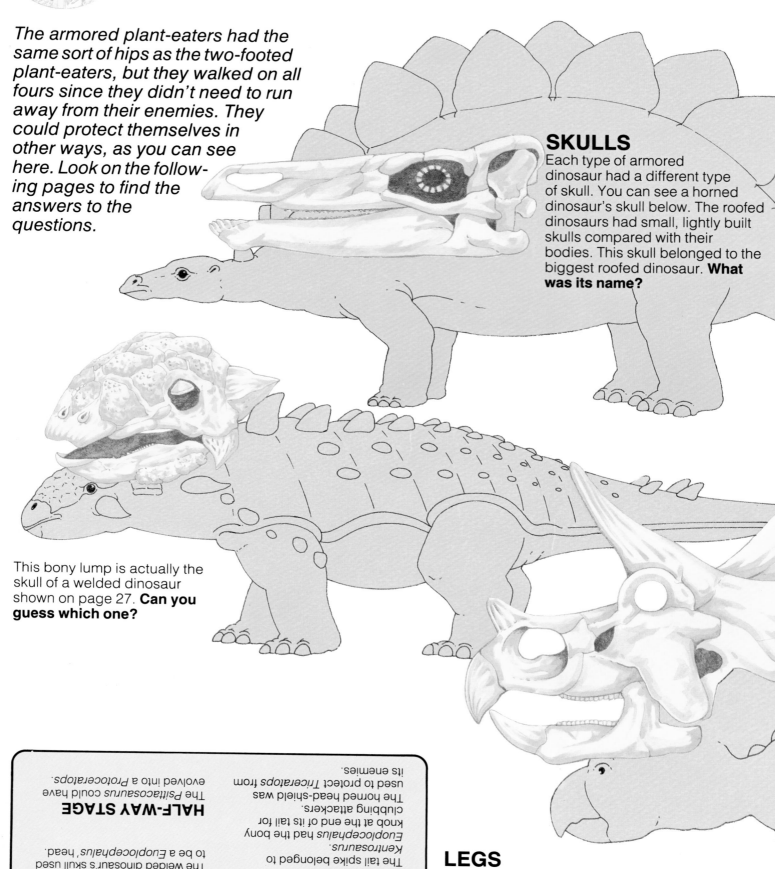

SKULLS

Each type of armored dinosaur had a different type of skull. You can see a horned dinosaur's skull below. The roofed dinosaurs had small, lightly built skulls compared with their bodies. This skull belonged to the biggest roofed dinosaur. **What was its name?**

This bony lump is actually the skull of a welded dinosaur shown on page 27. **Can you guess which one?**

LEGS

Like most of the big plant-eating dinosaurs, the armored dinosaurs had long hind legs and short front legs. This shows that they evolved from two-footed animals.

ANSWERS

SKULLS
The roofed dinosaur's skull once belonged to a Stegosaurus.
The welded dinosaur's skull used to be a Euoplocephalus' head.

WEAPONS
The tail spike belonged to Kentrosaurus.
Euoplocephalus had the bony knob at the end of its tail for clubbing attackers.
The horned head-shield was used to protect Triceratops from its enemies.

HALF-WAY STAGE
The Psittacosaurus could have evolved into a Protoceratops.

WEAPONS

As well as armor to protect themselves, these dinosaurs had weapons so that they could fight back.

The roofed dinosaurs had spikes on their tails, like this. **Look on the next page and see if you can guess which roofed dinosaur owned this.**

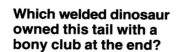

Which welded dinosaur owned this tail with a bony club at the end?

Which horned dinosaur had these forward-pointing horns on its head shield?

Make an armored plant-eater

Make the basic shape of a plant-eating animal by following the instructions here. Take a large lump of modeling clay and stick four half pencils into it for legs. Add a pencil tail at the back and a clay head at the front.

1. A large dinosaur this shape would be too heavy to run away from its enemies. It would have had to defend itself in some way. Cut up some pieces of cardboard to act as armor.

2. The backbone of most animals is the most vulnerable part of their bodies. Stick some armor plates along the backbone to keep away the meat-eaters' great jaws and teeth. All the "roofed dinosaurs" were armored like this.

3. We can take this type of armor further. Plaster the dinosaur's back with armor plates – like tiles on a floor. Cover the head with armor too. All the "welded dinosaurs" were armored like this.

4. A third way of armoring a dinosaur is to stick all the armor on its head. Then it can turn and face its enemies and protect the rest of its body. The "horned dinosaurs" were armored like this.

A HALF-WAY STAGE

Scientists think that a little dinosaur like this *Psittacosaurus* shows how two-footed plant-eaters (pages 20-23) turned into horned dinosaurs. The square shape of the head is produced by a bony ridge at the neck. This supported the neck and jaw muscles, and later evolved into the neck shield of the horned dinosaurs. **Which horned dinosaur do you think *Psittacosaurus* could have evolved into?**

Famous
armored plant-eaters

This is how big you would be, compared to the armored dinosaurs shown on this page.

Try to match up the ages and dates of each of these armored dinosaurs with the ages and dates of the meat-eaters on pages 14 and 15. Can you see which particular dinosaurs each one had to defend itself against?

Kentrosaurus (pointed lizard). This roofed dinosaur had spines along its back instead of plates. It was 17 feet (5 m) long and lived in East Africa in the late Jurassic.

Triceratops (three-horned head). This was the biggest and last of the horned dinosaurs. It was 30 feet (9 m) long and lived in North America at the very end of the Cretaceous.

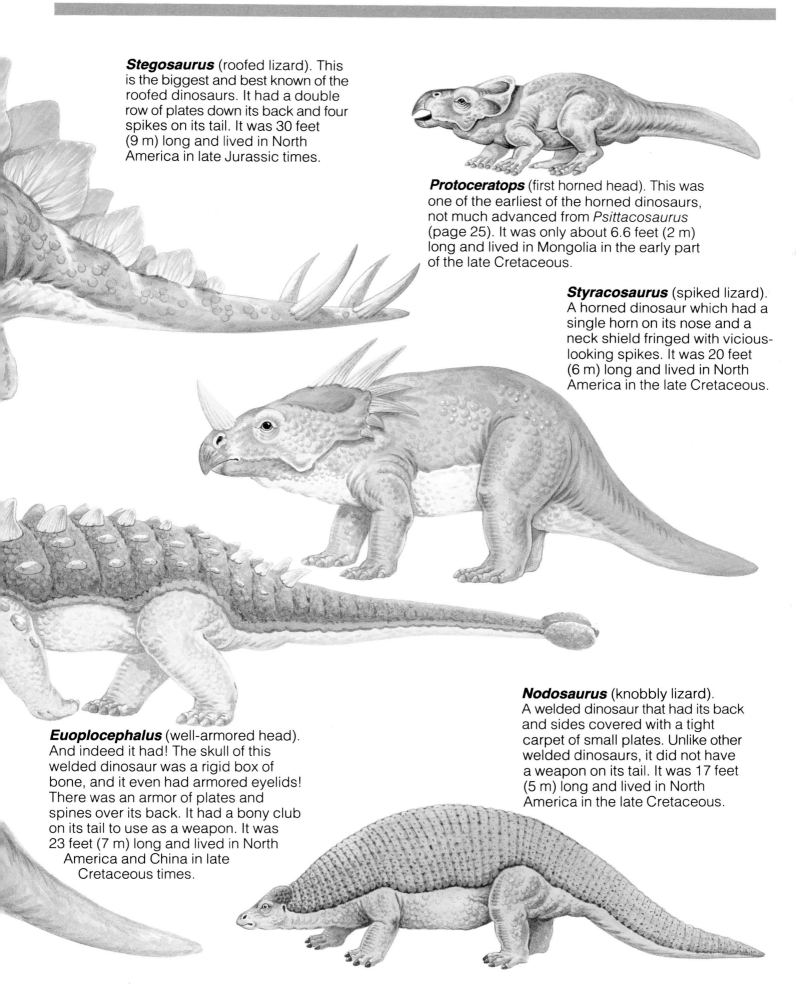

Stegosaurus (roofed lizard). This is the biggest and best known of the roofed dinosaurs. It had a double row of plates down its back and four spikes on its tail. It was 30 feet (9 m) long and lived in North America in late Jurassic times.

Protoceratops (first horned head). This was one of the earliest of the horned dinosaurs, not much advanced from *Psittacosaurus* (page 25). It was only about 6.6 feet (2 m) long and lived in Mongolia in the early part of the late Cretaceous.

Styracosaurus (spiked lizard). A horned dinosaur which had a single horn on its nose and a neck shield fringed with vicious-looking spikes. It was 20 feet (6 m) long and lived in North America in the late Cretaceous.

Euoplocephalus (well-armored head). And indeed it had! The skull of this welded dinosaur was a rigid box of bone, and it even had armored eyelids! There was an armor of plates and spines over its back. It had a bony club on its tail to use as a weapon. It was 23 feet (7 m) long and lived in North America and China in late Cretaceous times.

Nodosaurus (knobbly lizard). A welded dinosaur that had its back and sides covered with a tight carpet of small plates. Unlike other welded dinosaurs, it did not have a weapon on its tail. It was 17 feet (5 m) long and lived in North America in the late Cretaceous.

Flying animals

At the same time as the dinosaurs there lived some flying animals called "pterosaurs."

As with most animals, you can tell what pterosaurs ate by looking at their skulls and teeth. **See if you can match up the skulls with the pterosaurs opposite.**

(a) This big one had no teeth and probably ate fish, scooping them up from the sea's surface. Notice the long crest on its head.

This pterosaur had two kinds of teeth and probably ate meat.

(b)

(c) This skull belonged to one of the smallest pterosaurs. It may have eaten insects.

★ ANSWERS ★

Skull **(b)** was a *Dimorphodon's.*

Skull **(a)** belongs to *Pteranodon.*

Pterodactylus was the owner of skull **(c)**.

We can rebuild it!

This is the well-preserved fossil skeleton of a flying animal from the age of the dinosaurs.

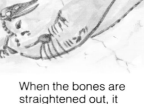

When the bones are straightened out, it gives a skeleton like this (a reconstruction).

We can then build up a picture of the animal like this (a restoration).

This flying animal's awkward name, *Rhamphorhynchus*, simply means "narrow beak." After we have found a well-preserved skeleton, it is easy to identify individual bones when we find them separately.

We can tell from the bones of *Rhamphorhynchus* and other pterosaurs that they were closely related to the dinosaurs. The crocodiles — still around today, of course — are related in the same way.

Make a pterosaur – or two!

Trace the outline shapes printed on pages 34 and 35. Cut the small single pteranodon out of the paper. Use some stiff cardboard to make the wings and body of the larger flyer.

1. Fold the small paper pterosaur along the dotted lines shown on the printed outline.
Staple the body together at the nose end. Make sure that the wings are straight and bent slightly upwards.

2. Gently launch this glider. If it flips down, turn up the feet slightly. If it flips up and then crashes, weight the nose with a piece of masking tape or two. A little bit of adjustment should get it flying nicely.

3. Fix a wing to each side of the large pterosaur's body with masking tape.
Make a hole in the center of each wing, about a third of the way along from the body. Attach a thread or a length of fishing line as shown and hang up the model.

4. To balance the model, put another piece of thread from the nose to the tail and add modeling clay until it makes the wings lie flat. This pterosaur should now flap its wings in a breeze.

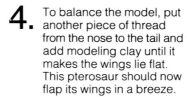

Which model do you think behaves most like a real pterosaur did – the glider or the flapper?
Scientists used to think that pterosaurs had a gliding flight. Now the experts have changed their minds and think that these flying reptiles flapped their wings like bats do. They think this because fossil pterosaur fur has been discovered – and it is just like a bat's.

Early bird

Pterosaurs were not birds, but the first birds were around at the same time. This bird is *Archaeopteryx*. It lived at the same time and in the same place as *Rhamphorhynchus* and *Pterodactylus*.

If you took the feathers away, it would look just like one of the small meat-eating dinosaurs – *Compsognathus*, shown on page 15. We think that the birds evolved from small meat-eaters like these.

Quetzalcoatlus was named after an ancient Mexican god – a flying snake. It was the biggest pterosaur known, with a wingspan of 40 feet (12 m) – as big as a light aircraft. It lived in North America in the late Cretaceous.

Pteranodon (winged with no teeth) had a hammer-head with a long crest balancing its toothless jaws. It had a wingspan of 26.5 feet (8 m) and lived in North America and Japan in the late Cretaceous.

Dimorphodon (two kinds of teeth). This was one of the earliest pterosaurs – its wingspan was 5 feet (1.5 m). It lived in southern England in early Jurassic times.

Pterodactylus (wing finger). This small short-tailed type of flying reptile may have been as small as a sparrow, with a wing span of less than 12 inches (30 cm). It lived in Europe in late Jurassic times.

Swimming reptiles

None of the dinosaurs actually lived in the sea. But many large sea reptiles did exist in the age of the dinosaurs. Here are a few of them.

PLESIOSAURS

These animals were described as "snakes threaded through the bodies of turtles." That was because their necks were long and thin for darting after prey, but their bodies were round and had paddle-like flippers. They probably "flew" through the water using their paddles like wings.

ICHTHYOSAURS

These were the fish-lizards, shaped just like fish so that they could live comfortably in water. They ate squid-like animals and fish.

PLACODONTS

These looked like big newts. Placodonts had strong crushing teeth for grinding up shellfish. They scraped them from the rocks with their front teeth. Some grew to look like sea turtles.

Elasmosaurus (long reptile). This was one of the longest, reaching 40 feet (12 m) long. It had over 70 vertebrae in its neck alone! It lived in North America and Japan in late Cretaceous times.

Ophthalmosaurus (eye lizard). This was one of the largest ichthyosaurs. It had big eyes that helped it to hunt but, unlike its smaller relatives, it had no teeth in its jaws. It was 10 feet (3 m) long and lived in Europe during the Jurassic period.

Placodus (flat-toothed) was a typical placodont. It was 6.6 feet (2 m) long and lived in Europe in middle Triassic times.

Make a plesiosaur

Build a plesiosaur and see how it worked. Make the body from a lump of modeling clay and stick cardboard paddles on each side. Make a head out of clay and a long neck from a piece of string. Now dangle it in the bath from threads, like a puppet. You will find that the body can move quite slowly, while the head can dart out to catch swift fish.

PLIOSAURS

These were the short-necked plesiosaurs and were big beasts – the whales of the Jurassic and Cretaceous seas. Like the sperm whale of today, they probably ate big squids and squid-like animals.

Kronosaurus (named after a giant in a Greek legend) was a giant of a pliosaur, about 56 feet (17 m) long, from the early Cretaceous of Australia. You would have been able to stand upright in its open jaws!

MOSASAURS

If you can imagine a crocodile living in the sea, with paddles instead of legs, that is what a mosasaur looked like. It was quite closely related to the lizards and snakes. Its triangular jaws were full of sharp strong teeth.

Tylosaurus was one of the biggest mosasaurs. It was 26.5 feet (8 m) long and lived in North America in late Cretaceous times.

Food

Here are some things that lived in the seas in Triassic, Jurassic, and Cretaceous times. **Can you work out which animals shown have eaten which of these foods?**

Leptolepis was a Jurassic fish like a herring. It would have swum swiftly away from any slow-moving enemy, unless that creature could suddenly dart after it.

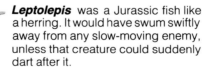

Belemnite A squid-like animal from the Jurassic and Cretaceous periods. It was probably eaten by toothless hunters.

Ammonite This was like a squid with a coiled shell. Fossil shells are sometimes found with tooth marks on them, showing where a strong-jawed animal had chewed them.

Terebratula was one of a group of shellfish called brachiopods. They were common in prehistoric times. Whole banks of them were probably good food for shell-eating animals.

Quiz time

True or False?

Some of these animals are real dinosaurs and really did exist. Others are completely made up. **Which ones do you think are true, and which false?**

1. *Spinosaurus*. A flesh-eating dinosaur from the early Cretaceous of West Africa. It has a big fin on its back, possibly to help it to keep cool.

2. *Chasmosaurus*. A horned plant-eater with an enormous frill. It lived in the late Cretaceous of North America.

3. *Pachycephalosaurus.* A two-footed plant-eater from the late Cretaceous of North America. It had a thick dome of bone on its head and may have used this against enemies as a battering ram.

4. *Aeolosaurus.* One of the welded dinosaurs, with a large, heavy body. Scientists have found skin impressions which show that it had gliding wings stretched between its legs. It lived in North Africa in late Jurassic times.

5. *Rhedosaurus*. A four-footed flesh-eater from the late Cretaceous of North America. It lived on other dinosaurs which it caught using its sharp teeth and claws.

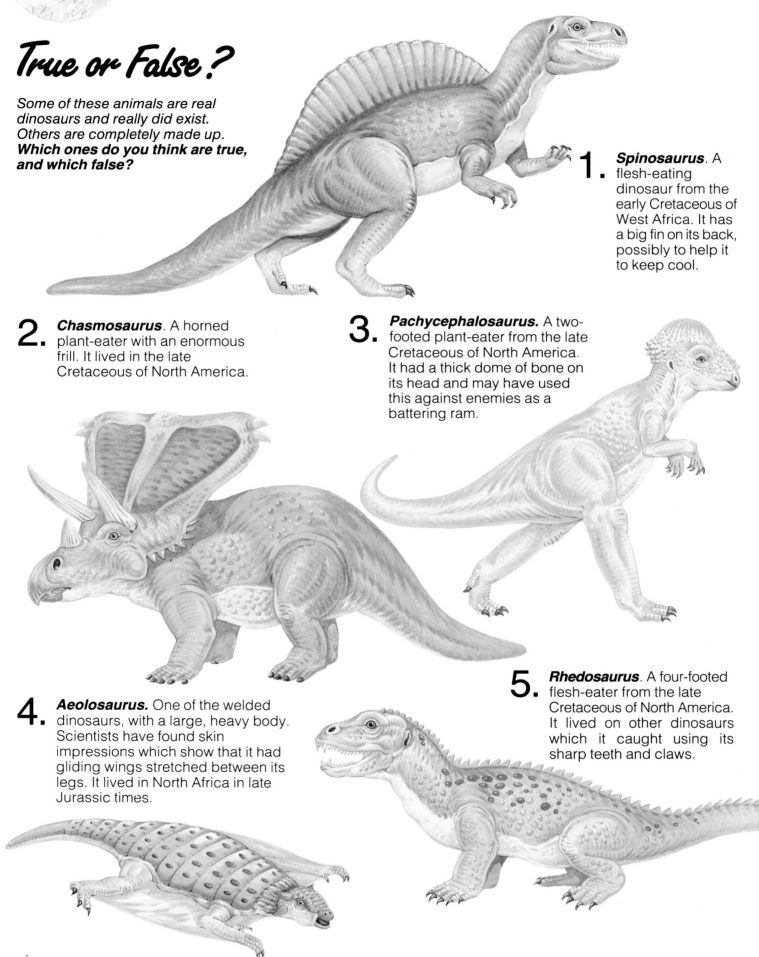

Open Wide

These teeth are from animals you have seen in this book. **Which ones do they belong to?**

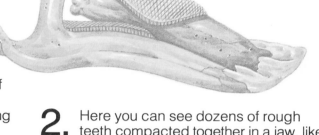

1. This is the roof of the mouth of a fossil reptile. The peg-like teeth at the front were for picking something off a rock, and the broad flat teeth on the palate must have been for crushing something very hard.

2. Here you can see dozens of rough teeth compacted together in a jaw, like kernels on a corncob. They must have been used for grinding down something tough, like pine-needles.

3. These leaf-like teeth belonged to a plant-eater as well. See how some of them have been worn down by chewing. The scientists who first found them thought that they looked like the teeth of the modern iguana lizard.

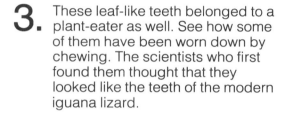

Who went there?

If you saw these footprints in a rock, what kind of dinosaur would you say made them?

1. These footprints were the size of serving trays and were made by one of the longest four-footed plant-eating dinosaurs.

2. These are from a two-footed animal. The footprints look a bit like birds' footprints. What do you think made that scrape up the middle?

3. These are from another two-footed animal. They have big claws on the toes.

★ ANSWERS ★

TRUE OR FALSE?

1. True. There were several finned flesh-eaters like this. The fin was supported on spines from the backbone.

2. True. The horned dinosaurs had frills that came in all sorts of shapes, and this was one of them.

3. True. The boneheads were a widespread group. They probably head-butted each other to see who would be the leader of the herd.

4. False. Any animal built like a fused dinosaur would have been far too heavy to fly.

5. False. There were no four-footed meat-eaters like this. They would not have been able to run fast enough to catch their food. This is a dinosaur invented for a monster film back in 1952.

WHO WENT THERE?

1. *Diplodocus*

2. A two-footed plant-eater — possibly *Iguanodon*. The mark up the middle is a tail scrape.

3. A meat-eater — possibly *Tyrannosaurus*.

OPEN WIDE

1. A placodont, such as *Placodus*, owned these teeth.

2. These are the teeth of a duck-bill, such as *Parasaurolophus*.

3. These teeth belong to *Iguanodon* — the name means "iguana-tooth."

Index

Glossary

Amphibian   An animal which lives as a tadpole in the water when young, but spends its adult life on land. Frogs and newts are amphibians.

Bed   A single layer of *sedimentary rock*.

Conifer   A cone-bearing tree. Conifers are usually evergreen, with needles instead of leaves.

Era   A large division of geological time, usually lasting tens of millions of years. Each era consists of a number of *periods*.

Fossil   The remains of a plant or animal found preserved in rock. Fossils are usually made of the hard parts of the animal or plant. The original material is often turned into stone. Footprints preserved in the rock are also fossils.

Horsetail   A primitive plant like a fern, with rings of narrow leaves growing from the joints of its stem.

Mammal   An animal that gives birth to live babies and then looks after them. Mammals are usually hairy.

Period   A division of geological time. Different animals lived during different periods. Experts can tell the periods apart by studying the different fossils that were formed during them.

Pterosaur   A flying reptile from the Mesozoic era. There were many types of pterosaur, but each had a furry body and leathery wings.

Reconstruction   The bones of a fossil animal, put together to form a skeleton.

Reptile   An animal that has a scaly skin and hatches from an egg on land. Lizards, snakes and crocodiles are reptiles. So were dinosaurs.

Restoration   A picture or a model made to show what a fossil animal would have looked like when it was alive.

Sedimentary rock   Rock made of layers of loose material, like sand or mud. The sand or mud was turned into rock by being buried and cemented together by minerals.

Skull   The structure of bones inside an animal's head, including the bones that make the brain-box, the face and the jaws.

Vertebra   One of the bones of the backbone, whether from the neck, the body or the tail. More than one vertebra are called vertebrae.

Vertebrate   Any animal with a backbone. Fish, amphibians, reptiles, birds and mammals are all vertebrates.